Anna, The Prophetess

Anna can hear God's voice and see glimpses of the future.
But when she receives dreams of a super-duper special Savior, her life takes an extraordinary turn!

A heartwarming picture book with tons of learning activities.

Learning Activities

The learning activities are designed to help grown ups engage children in meaningful discussions and activities while reading the book. Each activity is carefully crafted to reinforce important themes from the story and promote valuable life lessons. By choosing a different learning activity each time you read the book, you can guarantee a rich and educational experience for the children. By incorporating these learning activities into your reading, you can ensure that children not only enjoy the story but also learn valuable lessons about faith, patience, kindness, and trust in God's promises. These activities will make the reading experience fun, engaging, and educational, fostering important values in the young readers' lives.

Copyright 2023 Tokunbo Williams-Awhinawhi
All Rights reserved.

For my daughter, Anna, who fills my heart with joy each and every day. Greater works than these will you do.

All my love,
Mama

Content Page

- The story of Anna The Prophetess — 6
- Bible Reference & Fun Facts — 30
- Songs — 32
- Notes — 36
- Colouring — 38
- Letters — 44
- Making Angel Wings — 48
- Word find & Scramble — 50
- Maze & Fill in The Blanks — 52
- Prayers — 53
- Dream Journal — 54
- Create your own story — 58
- Notes — 68

There was a special girl named Anna who loved God a lot!

Anna had a super-duper special gift - she could hear God's voice and know about things before they happened.

That's why everyone called her Anna The Prophetess.

⭐

Learning Activity:

Discuss the character of Anna
- What was Anna's special gift?
- How do you think Anna felt when she heard God?
- Why was Anna called "Anna the Prophetess"?

Every morning, Anna talks to God, saying "Hello, God! It's me, Anna!"

Then, she reads her special book called the Bible.

And guess what? God talks back, saying, "I love you, Anna, and I'm always with you."

Anna feels really happy because God promised to be with her every single day.

Learning Activity:

Talking to God

Engage the children in a discussion about talking to God
- Why do you think Anna talks to God every morning?
- Why is it good to read your Bible every day?
- How do you think Anna feels when she hears God's response?

Phone Call to God

- If you have toy phones let the children pretend to call God, just like Anna does in the story. Encourage them to say "Hello, God! It's me, [their name]!" and then imagine God's response.

God would give Anna dreams of wonderful things that would happen later.

One night, in a dream, God whispered, "Anna, my dear, I have a surprise for the whole wide world. I'm sending a super-duper special Savior who will bring love to everyone."

When Anna woke up, she was so happy that she started dancing with joy!

Every night, Anna prayed for the special Savior to come quickly because she couldn't wait to meet him.

And each day, she waited for the Savior at the temple.

But, as time passed, she began to feel sad and wondered when the Savior would finally arrive.

Learning Activity:

Encourage patience and empathy

- Give the children small cards or pieces of paper. Ask them to write or draw a message of hope and encouragement that they would give to Anna during her time of waiting.
- Have the children share their waiting artwork, comfort items, and hopeful messages. Discuss the different ways they express their emotions and provide comfort to themselves or others.
- Encourage the children to remember Anna's waiting when they encounter situations that require patience.

Anna prayed to God again, asking for help.

And guess what? God sent His special angels to visit Anna.

These angels had shiny wings and big, happy faces! They said to Anna, "Don't be sad. Trust God! He always keeps His promises."

Learning Activity:

Role play

- Encourage the children to put on their angel wings and engage in a role-playing activity. Have them take turns being "angels" who deliver comforting messages to their friends.
- Discuss the themes of seeking help, receiving comfort, and trusting in promises. Remind the children that they can always ask for help from God and that His promises are trustworthy.

They said, "Anna, pretend you're a super-duper special tree by the river! When you trust God, you'll be as happy and strong as a tree with really deep roots that can stay firm in big storms. But if you don't trust God, you might blow away in the wind, whoosh, just like a tree without roots."

The angels also showed Anna special songs of hope and praise. They taught her how to sing them when she's feeling sad, to help her feel happier and to let God know that she trusts Him.

Learning Activity:

Discuss trust and resilience

- Encourage the children to talk about how they feel while the wind blows and discuss the importance of trust and deep roots (like the tree in the story) to stay strong during challenges.

Singing for Comfort

- Teach kids uplifting songs like "Jesus Loves Me."
- Sing together, use instruments or clapping for fun.
- Discuss the song's feelings and its ability to make everyone feel better
- Encourage singing when sad to foster trust and hope, like Anna's trust in God."

So, Anna didn't just sit and wait for the special Savior; she believed that God would keep His promise. Instead, she used her waiting time to help others.

One day, Anna saw a boy who got hurt near the temple.

Oh no! He looked very sad and in pain.

Learning Activity:

Promote kindness and helping

- Discuss with the children how they can make waiting time fun and use it as an opportunity to help others. Brainstorm simple acts of kindness they can perform while waiting, such as making cheerful cards, helping with chores, drawing pictures for someone, or sharing a smile with others.
- Remind the children that they have the power to make waiting time enjoyable for themselves and those around them by showing love and kindness

She hurried to him and held his hand. Anna knew that when she talked to God, good things would happen. So, she closed her eyes and prayed for him to feel better.

Quickly, the pain went away, and the boy hugged Anna really tight, saying, "Thank you, Anna!"

Anna learned something amazing - waiting and trusting God is fun!

Because she got to help others while waiting.

Waiting time becomes a fun time, being kind and helping others.

Learning Activity:

Promote kindness and helping

- Discuss with the children how they can make waiting time fun and use it as an opportunity to help others.
- Brainstorm simple acts of kindness they can perform while waiting, such as making cheerful cards, helping with chores, drawing pictures for someone, praying for someone or sharing a smile with others.
- Remind the children that they have the power to make waiting time enjoyable for themselves and those around them by showing love and kindness.

A while later, Anna saw a Baby named Jesus in the Temple. Her heart felt a flutter, and she heard God say, "This is the One, Anna. Jesus is the Savior I promised!"

At that special moment, Anna felt super-duper happy. She jumped, danced, and twirled around the Temple.

Anna thanked God for keeping His promise.

She sang songs of praise, and everyone joined in, thanking God together.

Learning Activity:

Reflection and connection with God

- Explain to the children that they will have the opportunity to explore their own connection with God.
- Provide drawing materials and encourage the children to find a quiet space to pray to God, asking Him to reveal a dream or vision to them, just as He did with Anna. They can ask for guidance, inspiration, or anything specific they would like to know.
- After praying, they should draw their dream or vision. Once finished ask them to share their dream and any special messages they received.
- As they share, emphasise the idea that dreams can be filled with wonderful surprises, just like Anna's dream about baby Jesus.
- Say a prayer of gratitude, thanking God for His faithfulness and for the promises He keeps. Encourage children to express their thanks in their own words.

LEARNING ACTIVITIES

Bible Reference

Luke chapter 2: verses 36-38
International Children's Bible

Anna Sees Jesus

Anna, a prophetess, was there at the Temple. She was from the family of Phanuel in the tribe of Asher. Anna was very old. She had once been married for seven years.

Then her husband died and she lived alone. She was now 84 years old. Anna never left the Temple. She worshiped God by fasting and praying day and night. She was standing there at that time, giving thanks to God. She talked about Jesus to all who were waiting for God to help Jerusalem.

Fun Facts

Anna's name means "grace" or "favor." It's a beautiful name that reflects how much God favored her.

Grace

She could hear messages from God and share them with others. It's like she had a special phone line to God!

Anna was a wise woman who lived to be 84 years old. That's a lot of birthdays and a lot of time to learn about life and God.

Anna is the New Testament's only named female prophetess

Anna would remain at the Temple constantly, living in continuous prayer and fasting

She was a daughter of Phanuel. She was a member of the tribe of Asher.

Jesus Loves Me

Jesus loves me! This I know,
For the Bible tells me so;
Little ones to Him belong,
They are weak but He is strong.
Yes, Jesus loves me!
Yes, Jesus loves me!
The Bible tells me so.

Jesus loves me! He who died,
Heaven's gate to open wide;
He will wash away my sin,
Let His little child come in.
Yes, Jesus loves me!
Yes, Jesus loves me!
The Bible tells me so.

Jesus loves me! loves me still,
When I'm very weak and ill;
From His shining throne on high,
Comes to watch me where I lie.
Yes, Jesus loves me!
Yes, Jesus loves me!
The Bible tells me so.

Jesus loves me! He will stay,
Close beside me all the way;
He's prepared a home for me,
And some day His face I'll see.
Yes, Jesus loves me!
Yes, Jesus loves me!
The Bible tells me so

He's Got the Whole World in His Hands

He's got the whole world in his hands.
He's got the whole wide world in his hands.
He's got the whole world in his hands.
He's got the whole world in his hands.

He's got the wind and the rain in his hands.
He's got the wind and the rain in his hands.
He's got the wind and the rain in his hands.
He's got the whole world in his hands.

He's got the little bitty baby in his hands.
He's got the little bitty baby in his hands.
He's got the little bitty baby in his hands.
He's got the whole world in his hands.

He's got you and me sister in his hands.
He's got you and me sister in his hands.
He's got you and me sister in his hands.
He's got the whole world in his hands.

He's got everybody in his hands.
He's got everybody in his hands.
He's got everybody in his hands.

He's got the whole world in his hands.

The Lord's Prayer

OUR FATHER IN HEAVEN,
Remember that the God who loves us like a parent created everything and wants us to know and love him

HALLOWED BE YOUR NAME,
Thank God for your family and friends, for Jesus, for God's love, or for the world, our home.

YOUR KINGDOM COME,
Pray for God to make the world better and fix things. For peace, fairness, and for no more hunger or sickness. Think about people who really need God's help, and ask God to watch over them.

YOUR WILL BE DONE, ON EARTH AS IN HEAVEN.
*Pray for people to do the things that make God happy
Ask for God to help you understand what you should do and for the help to do it.*

GIVE US TODAY OUR DAILY BREAD.
Pray for what you need and also the needs of your family, friends, and community.

FORGIVE US OUR SINS AS WE FORGIVE THOSE WHO SIN AGAINST US.
*Ask God to forgive you for all the things you've done wrong. Ask for God's help you be more patient and forgiving towards others.
Is there someone you need God's help to forgive?*

SAVE US FROM THE TIME OF TRIAL
Ask for God's help with the things that make your life hard, things that upset you, and things that make it hard for you to do what's right.

AND DELIVER US FROM EVIL.
Ask for God to protect you and others from evil.

FOR THE KINGDOM, THE POWER, AND THE GLORY ARE YOURS NOW AND FOR EVER.
Give glory to God for creating all things

AMEN.

Prayers

THANK YOU GOD FOR THE WORLD SO SWEET,
THANK YOU GOD FOR THE FOOD WE EAT,
THANK YOU GOD FOR THE BIRDS THAT SING,
THANK YOU GOD FOR EVERYTHING!
AMEN

DEAR GOD,

THANK YOU FOR THIS DAY,
FOR GUIDING US ALONG THE WAY.
PLEASE KEEP US SAFE, BOTH NIGHT AND DAY,
AS WE LEARN, GROW, AND PLAY.

HELP US BE KIND, LOVING, AND TRUE,
TO SHARE OUR JOY AND HELP OTHERS TOO.
WITH YOUR LOVE, WE'LL FIND OUR WAY,
IN ALL WE DO, WE'LL TRUST AND OBEY.

AMEN.

NOTES

NOTES

Colouring

Colouring

Colouring

Colouring

Colouring

Colouring

Write a letter to Anna

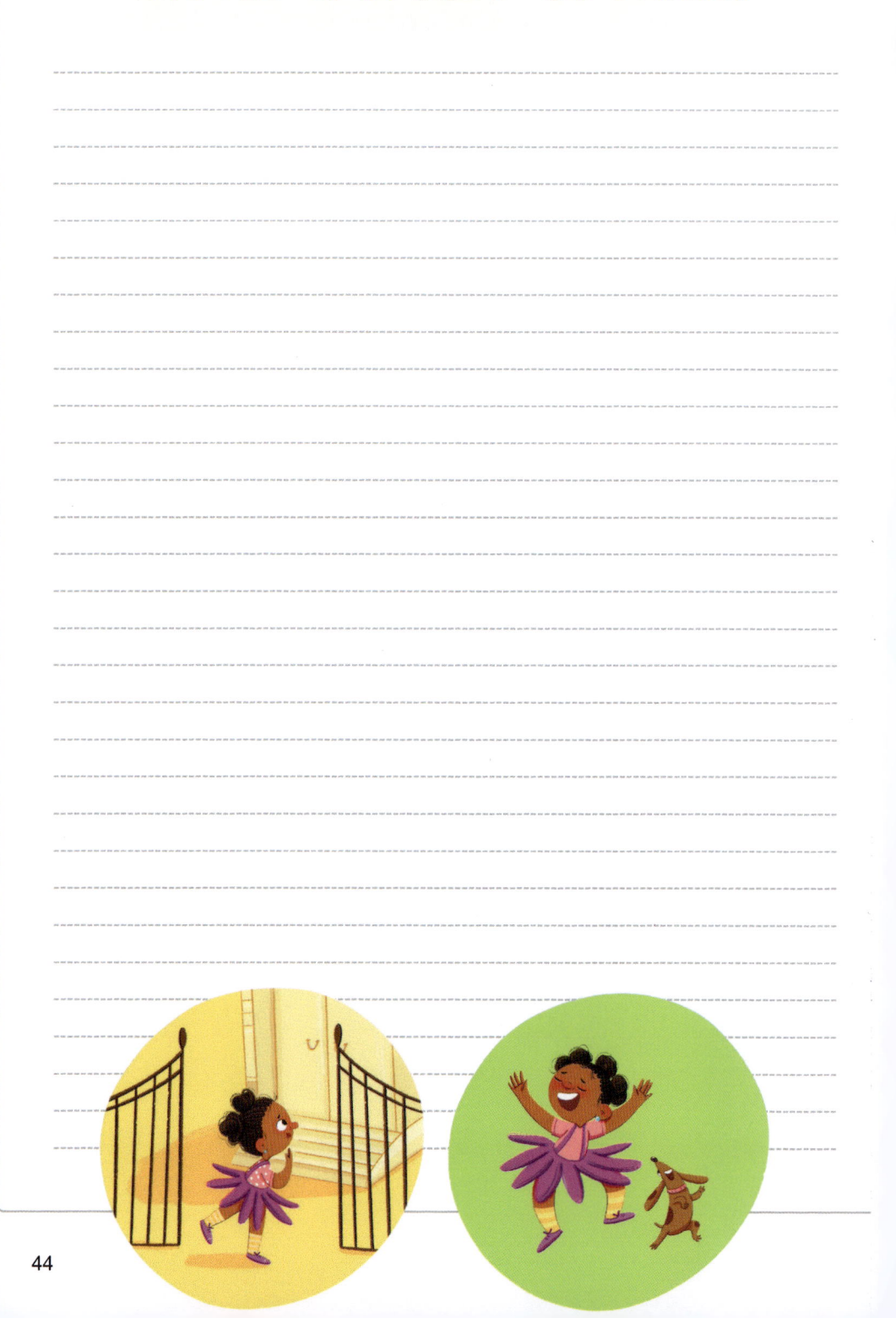

Write a letter to Jesus

Write a letter to the Angels

Write a letter to God

Making Angel Wings

Are you ready to create your very own angel wings? It's a fun and creative craft that you can do with some simple materials. Here's how to make your angel wings step by step:

What You'll Need:
- White poster board or cardboard
- A pencil
- Scissors (with adult supervision)
- Glue or tape
- Soft and fluffy white feathers
- Elastic cord or pretty ribbon
- Decorations like glitter, sequins, or paint for sparkle!

Let's Get Started

Step 1: Prepare Your Workspace
- Find a clean and spacious area to work on. Make sure you have enough space to spread out your materials and work comfortably.

Step 2: Draw the Wing Shape
- Take your white poster board or cardboard and decide how big you want your angel wings to be. They can be as big or as small as you like!
- Use a pencil to draw the shape of one wing. Think of it like a big teardrop with a curved top.
- Carefully cut out the wing shape you just drew. This will be your pattern for the second wing.

Step 3: Create the Second Wing
- Put your first wing shape on another piece of poster board or cardboard.
- Trace around it to make the second wing.
- Cut out the second wing so that you have a matching pair of wings.

Making Angel Wings

Step 4: Decorate the Wings
- If you want your angel wings to shine and sparkle, you can use glitter, sequins, or paint to decorate them. Make them look as angelic as you like!

Step 5: Attach the Feathers
- Turn your wings over so that the side without decorations is facing up.
- Put glue or tape along the curved top of one wing.
- Carefully press the soft, white feathers onto the glue or tape. Overlap the feathers slightly to make them look fluffy. Repeat this step for the second wing.

Step 6: Attach Elastic Cord or Ribbon
- Flip your wings over again so that the feathered side is facing down.
- Take a piece of elastic cord or pretty ribbon and measure it to fit around your shoulders comfortably.
- Attach one end of the cord or ribbon to the top edge of one wing using glue or tape.
- Do the same thing for the other wing, making sure the cord or ribbon is evenly spaced between the two wings.

Step 7: Secure the Wings
- Wait for the glue to dry completely. This will make sure your wings are nice and secure.

Step 8: Have Fun!
- Now it's time to put on your angel wings! Slip your arms through the cord or ribbon loops. Your wings should rest comfortably on your back like a backpack.
- Use your imagination and have fun pretending to be an angel. You can dress-up or wear your wings to a special event or costume party!

Remember to be careful with scissors and glue!

Word Find

G	D	O	U	E	F	D	F	U	A	A	T	U	R
R	N	O	K	N	U	P	N	D	J	E	S	U	S
S	I	O	G	S	E	P	D	T	N	K	P	G	S
R	K	N	S	G	L	I	N	S	G	I	F	T	V
S	R	M	S	O	A	N	N	A	J	G	A	N	R
S	R	A	U	J	N	R	D	J	S	N	J	S	N
E	D	E	P	T	M	G	S	A	A	N	R	R	G
M	P	F	E	L	R	E	M	E	T	O	G	R	N
O	G	N	R	T	R	S	D	D	R	E	A	M	N
N	T	R	D	A	L	R	N	A	T	K	O	E	R
N	I	O	U	S	O	T	S	S	R	G	N	T	S
S	D	S	P	M	V	T	U	G	O	G	D	I	O
I	N	S	E	I	E	R	A	S	G	D	A	P	G
G	N	U	R	R	T	S	U	R	D	G	O	D	O

JESUS   **SUPERDUPER**   **ANNA**
TRUST   **GOD**   **LOVE**
SONG   **DREAM**   **GIFT**

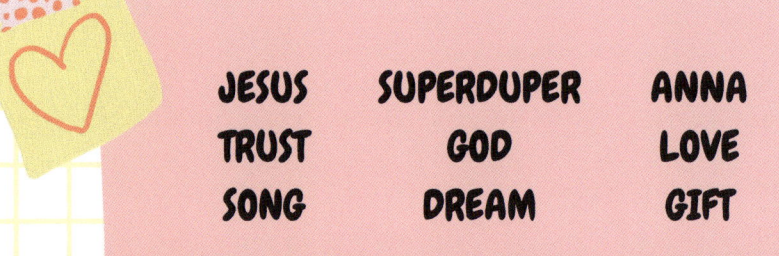

Word Scramble

1. EOVL _____
2. ANAN _____
3. ESSUJ _____
4. ODG _____
5. EANLG _____
6. TSRTU _____
7. NOSG _____
8. DKIN _____
9. SUEPR _____
10. DPEUR _____
11. SPIAECL _____
12. SAOVIUR _____

words to find

LOVE	ANGEL	SUPER
ANNA	TRUST	DUPER
JESUS	SONG	SPECIAL
GOD	KIND	SAVIOUR

Anna's Maze

Fill in the Blanks

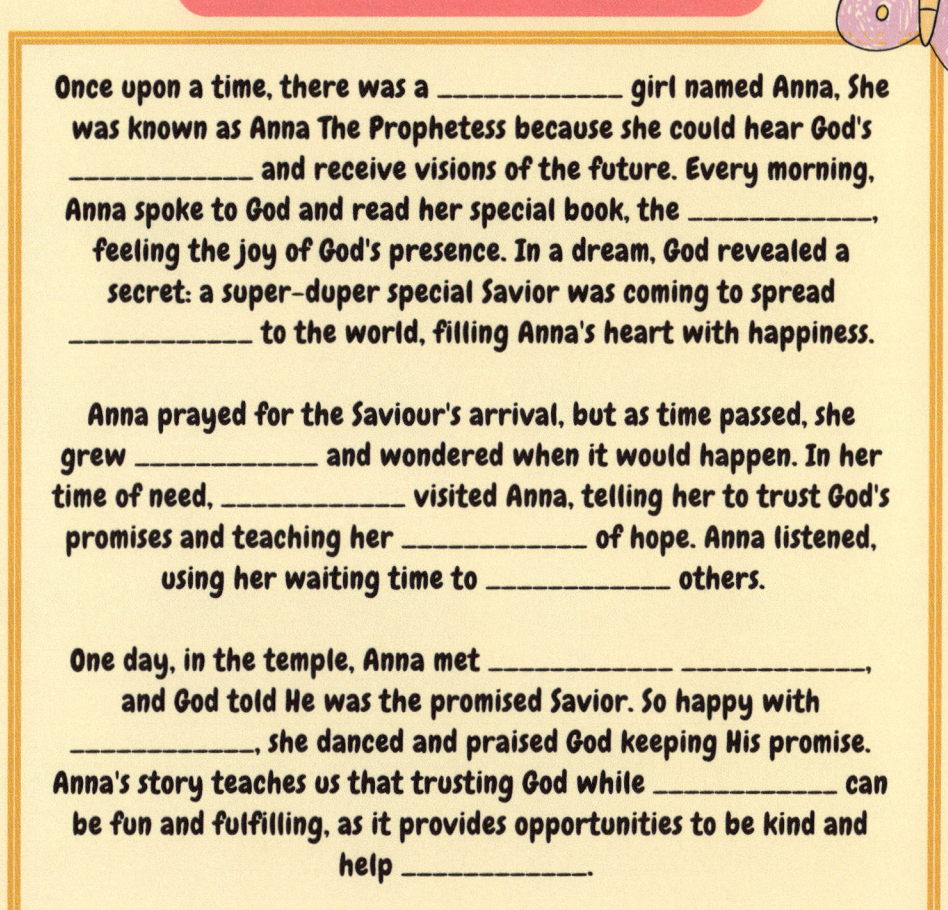

Once upon a time, there was a _____ girl named Anna, She was known as Anna The Prophetess because she could hear God's _____ and receive visions of the future. Every morning, Anna spoke to God and read her special book, the _____, feeling the joy of God's presence. In a dream, God revealed a secret: a super-duper special Savior was coming to spread _____ to the world, filling Anna's heart with happiness.

Anna prayed for the Saviour's arrival, but as time passed, she grew _____ and wondered when it would happen. In her time of need, _____ visited Anna, telling her to trust God's promises and teaching her _____ of hope. Anna listened, using her waiting time to _____ others.

One day, in the temple, Anna met _____ _____, and God told He was the promised Savior. So happy with _____, she danced and praised God keeping His promise. Anna's story teaches us that trusting God while _____ can be fun and fulfilling, as it provides opportunities to be kind and help _____.

Words to Choose From:

1. Special
2. Voice
3. Bible
4. Love
5. Sad
6. Angels
7. Songs
8. Help
9. Baby Jesus
10. Joy
11. Waiting
12. Others

Dream Journal: Draw or write about your dreams or things you hope for in the future.

Dream Journal: Draw or write about your dreams or things you hope for in the future.

Dream Journal: Draw or write about your dreams or things you hope for in the future.

Dream Journal: Draw or write about your dreams or things you hope for in the future.

Draw & Write

write your own short short stories about anything, Anna, Your family, your friends or God!

Draw & Write

write your own short short stories about anything, Anna, Your family, your friends or God!

Draw & Write

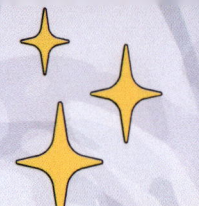

write your own short short stories about anything, Anna, Your family, your friends or God!

Draw & Write

write your own short short stories about anything, Anna, Your family, your friends or God!

Draw & Write

write your own short short stories about anything, Anna, Your family, your friends or God!

Draw & Write

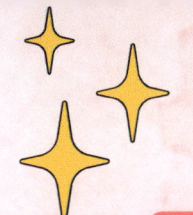

write your own short short stories about anything, Anna, Your family, your friends or God!

Draw & Write

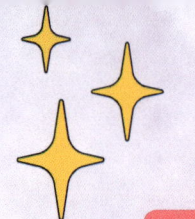

write your own short short stories about anything, Anna, Your family, your friends or God!

Draw & Write

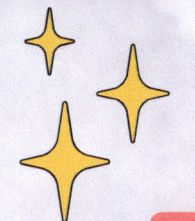

write your own short short stories about anything, Anna, Your family, your friends or God!

Draw & Write

write your own short short stories about anything, Anna, Your family, your friends or God!

Draw & Write

write your own short short stories about anything, Anna, Your family, your friends or God!

NOTES

NOTES

NOTES

NOTES

NOTES

NOTES

Anna, The Prophetess

Learning Activities

The learning activities are designed to help grown ups engage children in meaningful discussions and activities
while reading the book. Each activity is carefully crafted to reinforce important themes from the story and promote valuable
life lessons. By choosing a different learning activity each time you read the book, you can guarantee a rich and educational experience for the children. By
incorporating these learning activities into your reading, you can ensure that children not only enjoy the story but also learn valuable lessons about faith, patience, kindness, and trust in God's promises. These activities will make the reading experience
fun, engaging, and educational, fostering important values in the young readers' lives.

Author
Tokunbo Williams-Awhinawhi

Illustrator
Sveta Sadykova

Copyright 2023 Tokunbo Williams-Awhinawhi
All Rights reserved.

Printed in Great Britain
by Amazon

0050278a-7c44-4955-a6bb-3b52ec38783bR01